CIRCUIT CLAY

BY THE EDITORS OF KLUTZ

KLUTZ®

KLUTZ® creates activity books and other great stuff for kids ages 3 to 103. We began our corporate life in 1977 in a garage we shared with a Chevrolet Impala. Although we've outgrown that first office, Klutz galactic headquarters is still staffed entirely by real human beings. For those of you who collect mission statements, here's ours:

CREATE WONDERFUL THINGS • BE GOOD • HAVE FUN

LEDs and battery case manufactured in China. All other parts, Korea. 91

WRITE US
We would love to hear your comments regarding this or any of our books.
KLUTZ®
568 Broadway, Suite 503
New York, NY 10012
thefolks@klutz.com

Distributed in Australia by
Scholastic Australia Ltd
PO Box 579
Gosford, NSW
Australia 2250

Distributed in Hong Kong by
Scholastic Hong Kong Ltd
Suites 2001-2, Top Glory Tower
262 Gloucester Road
Causeway Bay, Hong Kong

Distributed in Canada by
Scholastic Canada Ltd
604 King Street West
Toronto, Ontario
Canada M5V 1E1

ISBN 978-1-338-10636-7

4 1 5 8 5 7 0 8 8 8

MIX
Paper from responsible sources
FSC® C023083
www.fsc.org

We make Klutz books using resources that have been approved by the Forest Stewardship Council®. This means the paper in this book comes exclusively from trees that have been grown and harvested responsibly.

Photos © Fotolia: case, box, interior circuit background (Amgun); box front circuit background (stockchairatgfx).

CONTENTS

⚡ = **DIFFICULTY LEVEL**

WHAT YOU GET

You get 4 colors of conductive clay in blue, green, orange, and black. To learn more about your conductive clay, turn to page 8.

The white clay in your kit is insulating clay. You'll use both conductive and insulating clay in your projects—see page 14 for more info. This clay is firmer than your colored clay, so you'll have to knead it more to soften it.

20 LEDs in 5 colors will light up your circuit clay projects. Read **LED CARE** on page 6 before you start using LEDs.

Your battery pack will power your circuit projects. Read **POWER UP** on page 7 before you start your using your pack.

Use the paper punch-outs to add fun details to your clay sculptures. Turn to page 9 to learn how to use them.

HOW THIS BOOK WORKS

This book teaches you how to make clay sculptures that light up. Be sure to read **BEFORE YOU START** on pages 6–7 first so you'll know what you need for your projects. Start with the projects on pages 10–16 to learn how to build a basic circuit and use insulating clay. Then try a few of the projects on pages 18–51 before you start making your own clay creations.

OTHER STUFF YOU'LL NEED

- **4 AA batteries**
- **Dental floss:** to cut clay easily
- **Toothpick and pencil:** to shape the clay
- **Colored pencils, markers, and pens:** to color in the paper punch-outs
- **Paper towels:** for clean-up
- **Resealable plastic bag or container:** to store your clay

BEFORE YOU START

SETTING UP YOUR WORKSPACE

- Choose a flat surface that's easy to wipe clean, like a table or desk. Wash your hands with soap and water before and after you use the clay to keep things clean.

- The clay may rub off on fabrics, so wear old clothes or a smock.

- Keep your clay in a resealable plastic bag or container so it won't dry out.

CLEANING UP

- Your clay sculptures won't work if you let the clay dry out. After you're done crafting, remove the wires, LEDs, and battery pack from your clay sculptures. Use a paper towel to clean the clay off the LED legs and wire ends.

- Put the clay in a resealable plastic bag or container to keep it from drying out.

- Keep your supplies away from babies and pets.

LED CARE

- Never touch the battery pack wires directly to LED legs. You'll burn out the LED and it won't light up anymore. Light LEDs only when they're in a circuit with clay.

- Bend LED legs very gently. The legs can break easily. If a whole leg breaks off, throw the LED out.

- If you want more LEDs, they're easy to find in electronics stores. Just look for 5 mm LEDs.

POWER UP:
YOUR BATTERY PACK

- You'll need an adult to help you with the battery pack. Have the adult read **BATTERY INSTRUCTIONS FOR ADULTS** on page 2 before starting any activities.

- You'll need four AA batteries to power your projects. Have an adult remove the screw in the lid of the case to install the batteries. Be sure to place the positive and negative ends of the batteries in the case correctly and to put the screw back in the lid.

- There's an ON/OFF switch on the pack. Keep it switched to OFF when you're crafting or not using the battery pack.

- When you're done crafting, have the adult remove the batteries from the pack.

- The ends of the black and red wires on your pack should have a little bit of metal wire sticking out. If a metal tip breaks off, have an adult use nail clippers to carefully cut off the black or red plastic around the end of the metal wire.

- Use the battery pack and LEDs only for the crafts in this book.

- Never touch the ends of the red and black wires together or you'll drain the battery.

CLAY BASICS

SHAPING

Ball

Tear off a chunk of clay about the size you want the ball to be. Roll the clay in a circle between your hands until it's a ball. To make a tiny ball, roll the clay between your pointer finger and thumb.

Cone

Use a finger to roll one side of a clay ball. Roll it back and forth a few times.

Triangle

Use your fingers to shape a ball into a rough triangle. Press the clay against the table to make flat sides.

Snake

Roll a clay ball back and forth with two fingers. To make your snake an even thickness, roll your fingers up and down the shape evenly.

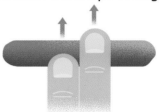

Cubes & Rectangles

Take a clay ball and press it against the table to make a flat side. Turn the ball over and make another flat side. Repeat until you have six flat sides and your ball looks like a block.

Flattening

To make a shape flat, just press it against the table. To make it thinner, turn it over and press it again.

HOW MUCH CLAY SHOULD I USE?

The instructions for each project will tell you what size clay ball you need to start with. As you start your projects, roll your clay into balls and place them over the pictures below to check their sizes. You can always add or take away clay to make your balls the right size.

LARGE

MEDIUM

SMALL

TINY

PAPER PUNCH-OUTS

Your book comes with two sheets of paper punch-outs to decorate your clay sculptures. Gently remove a punch-out from the sheet by poking it with a finger. Push the tabs into the clay to attach them to a finished sculpture. If a tab has dotted lines, that means you'll fold it first before adding it to the clay. Some of the punch-outs are black-and-white so you can color them in to make your projects unique.

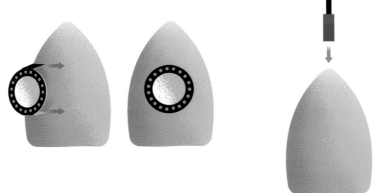

Don't let your clay dry out!

Your clay circuits won't work if the clay is dried out—think of them as temporary pieces of art. After you're done experimenting, take out the wires, LEDs, and punch-outs, and put your clay in a resealable plastic bag to keep it moist. In case your clay does dry out, wrap it in a damp paper towel and place it in a resealable plastic bag overnight.

Here's how to build your very first clay circuit.

WHAT YOU'LL NEED:

- Green clay
- LED
- Battery pack
- 4 AA batteries

1 Make two cubes from two medium balls of green clay.

2 Look at the wires or "legs" on your LED. One leg is a little longer—this is the positive ⊕ leg. The shorter leg is the negative ⊖ leg.

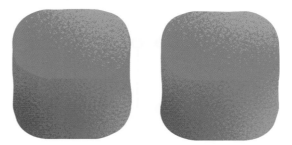

NEGATIVE (SHORTER LEG) ⊖

POSITIVE (LONGER LEG) ⊕

3 Gently split the legs so they angle out. Stick the positive ⊕ leg into the clay cube on the left. Stick the negative ⊖ leg into the clay cube on the right. Keep the cubes separated.

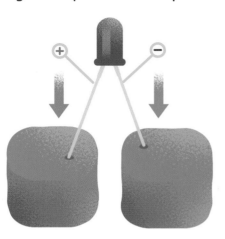

4 Have an adult put 4 AA batteries in your battery case. (Pssst! Tell your grown-up to take out the screw first and put it back in once the batteries are in.) Make sure the switch on the case is OFF.

5 Your battery case has two wires—the red wire is positive ⊕ and the black wire is negative ⊖.

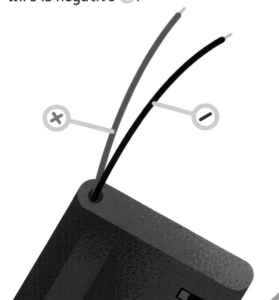

6 Stick the end of the red wire into the clay cube on the left. Stick the end of the black wire into the clay cube on the right. Switch the battery case to ON. Watch the LED light up. You've created a circuit!

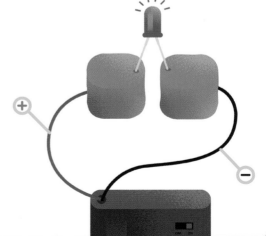

WHAT'S A CIRCUIT?

A circuit is a loop that allows an electric current to flow through it. The circuit that you just built on pages 10-11 has four basic parts:

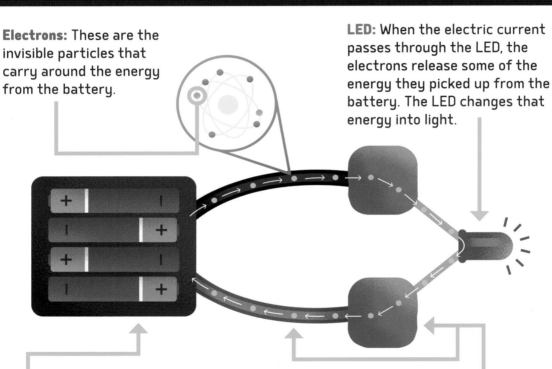

Electrons: These are the invisible particles that carry around the energy from the battery.

LED: When the electric current passes through the LED, the electrons release some of the energy they picked up from the battery. The LED changes that energy into light.

Battery: The battery provides energy to the electrons. After the electrons release some of their energy, they return to the battery for more. Electrons travel in only one direction—they always flow from the negative end of the battery to the positive end.

Wires and clay: The wires and the clay allow your electrons to travel through the electric circuit. You'll use wires and clay to connect the parts of your circuit together.

WHAT MAKES CLAY CONDUCTIVE?

The blue, green, orange, and black clays in your kit are made of ingredients that allow the electrons in the electric current to flow through them.

When a material is conductive, it means that the electrons in an electric current can move through it. The colored clay that comes with the book has lots of "free" electrons. A free electron is an electron that's loosely bonded to its atom and can move around. These free electrons are what allow the electric current to flow through the clay.

ZAP IT TO ME!

So what is electricity? When a bunch of electrons start moving in the same direction, they create an electric current. These electrons carry and release energy from your battery to power your LED and make it light up.

HOW INSULATING CLAY WORKS

WHAT YOU'LL NEED:

- **Basic circuit (page 10)**
- **White insulating clay**

1 Take the circuit you built on pages 10–11 and turn the switch on so that the LED lights up.

2 Move the clay cubes together until they touch. The LED should go out.

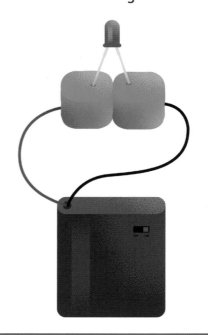

? WHY DID THE LIGHT GO OUT?

What happened? By touching the clay cubes together, you created a short circuit. A short circuit happens when you make another path that's easier for the electric current to travel though. To learn more about short circuits, turn to page 16.

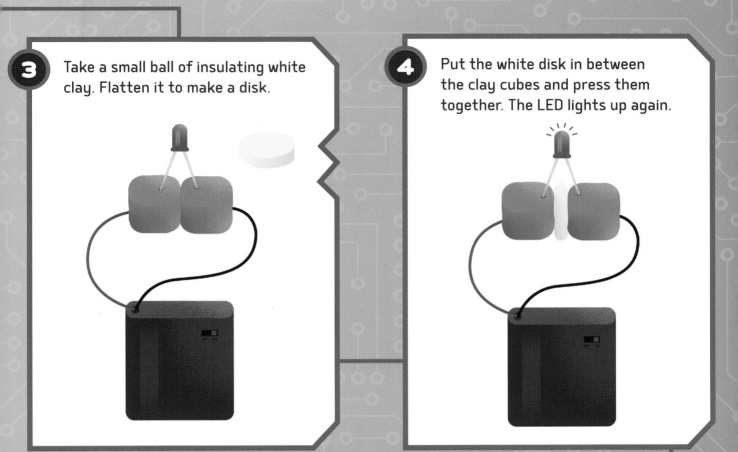

3 Take a small ball of insulating white clay. Flatten it to make a disk.

4 Put the white disk in between the clay cubes and press them together. The LED lights up again.

? WHY DOES THE LED LIGHT UP NOW?

Your white clay is different from the blue, orange, green, and black clay in your kit. This clay is an insulator, which means electric current can't flow through it. Turn the page to learn more about your white insulating clay.

WHAT IS A SHORT CIRCUIT?

Remember how we said a circuit was like a loop? Think of a short circuit as a shortcut. Though electrons are good at carrying energy in an electric current, they're kind of lazy. They'll take the shortest path around a circuit and skip anything that makes them work, such as lighting up an LED. By touching the clay cubes together in your basic circuit, you made a way for the electrons to flow through the circuit without going through the LED.

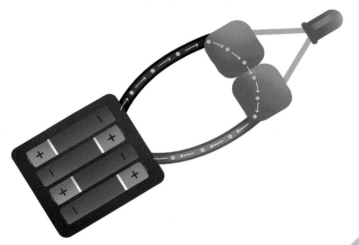

How does white insulating clay work?
The white insulating clay in your kit doesn't allow an electric current to flow through it. When you added the insulating clay to your short circuit on page 15, you blocked the shortcut through the clay cubes. Without the shortcut, the electrons have no choice but to go through the LED and light it up as they flow through the circuit loop.

TEST YOUR CIRCUITS!

When you see this symbol in your project instructions, switch ON your battery pack to see if your LEDs light up. If they don't, take a look at the Troubleshooting tips on the next page to fix your circuit before you go on to the next step.

TROUBLESHOOTING

Are you making a project but your LEDs aren't lighting up?
Run through this checklist to find solutions to some common clay
circuit problems.

☐ Check to see if your battery pack is turned ON. Have an adult
check that your batteries work and are inserted properly.

☐ The clay with the positive LED legs and the clay with the negative
LED legs shouldn't touch (that creates a short circuit). Your
project instructions will say which clay parts shouldn't touch, so
double-check that everything is correct.

☐ Try swapping the two legs of the black wire and the red wire
where they plug into the clay. If that fixes the problem, you just
mixed up the positions of the positive and negative LED legs.

☐ If not all the LEDs light up, take out the ones that don't work. Turn
the LED around and switch the positive and negative legs. Put the
LED back into the clay to see if that works.

☐ It's possible that your LED is burned out. Make a basic circuit
(page 10) with the LED to check. Be sure to pay attention to where
the positive and negative legs and wires go.

REMEMBER

The important thing to keep in mind when working with clay circuits
is that the electric current needs to flow through your sculpture in
a loop from the black wire in the battery pack to the red wire in the
battery pack. Try the projects on pages 18–51 to practice, then try
making your own original sculptures.

WHAT YOU'LL NEED:

- Green clay
- Orange clay
- White insulating clay
- Red LED
- Paper punch-outs: 2 rocket wings, window, antenna

1 Shape two small green clay balls into cubes to make rocket boosters. Lay down your LED so that the positive ⊕ leg is on the left. Curl the LED legs in and bend them upward, like wings.

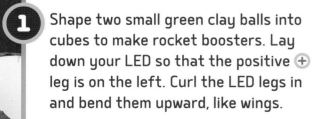

2 Flip the LED upside down. Push one LED leg down into each of the green boosters. Remember to keep the positive ⊕ leg on the left.

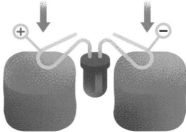

3 Shape a small ball of white clay into a thin rectangle. Press it over the boosters to hide the LED legs. Make sure the boosters don't touch each other.

4 For the rocket's body, roll a large orange clay ball into a football shape. Flatten one end on the table to make a rounded cone.

5 Insert the paper punch-outs to add wings, a window, and an antenna to your rocket. Place the body on top of the white rectangle.

6 Make sure the orange body doesn't touch the green boosters. Push the red battery wire into the left booster. Push the black battery wire into the right booster.

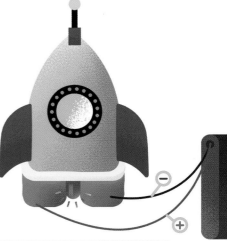

TEST YOUR CIRCUIT NOW!

UFO

WHAT YOU'LL NEED:

- Green clay
- White insulating clay
- 4 LEDs
- Paper punch-outs: alien, antenna

1 Shape a medium green ball into a thick disk by flattening it a little.

2 Roll a small white clay ball into a snake. Flatten it to make a strip. Wrap the strip around the green disk.

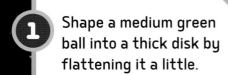

3 Roll a large green ball into a thick snake. Wrap it around the white strip.

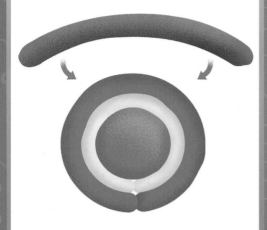

4 Insert the LEDs around the top. Stick the shorter, negative ⊖ legs into the green center. Push the longer, positive ⊕ legs into the outer green circle. Connect the battery pack by sticking the black wire ⊖ into the green center disk. Poke the red wire ⊕ into the outer green circle.

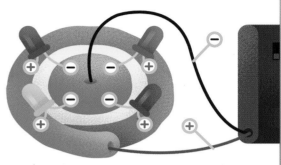

TEST YOUR CIRCUIT NOW!

5 Roll a large white clay ball into an egg shape. Press the bottom of the egg flat to make a dome.

6 Add the paper alien and the antenna to the dome. Lay the dome on the center, over the black wire. If you want, add small clay dots around the outside of your UFO to spiff it up.

WHAT YOU'LL NEED:

- Black clay
- White insulating clay
- Orange clay
- Green clay
- 2 LEDs
- Paper punch-outs: 2 butterfly wings, bumblebee
- Optional: Pencil, toothpick

1 Flatten a medium black ball slightly. Use the point of a pencil to make dots all over the clay.

2 Roll a small ball of white clay into a thin snake. Wrap it around the flower center.

3 Roll small orange clay balls, then flatten them into ovals for petals. If you want, press the side of a toothpick into the petals to add grooves. Place the petals around the black center and make sure the petal edges touch each other.

4 Insert the shorter negative ⊖ LED legs into the flower center, and the longer positive ⊕ legs into the petals. Poke the red wire ⊕ into a petal and the black wire ⊖ into the center.

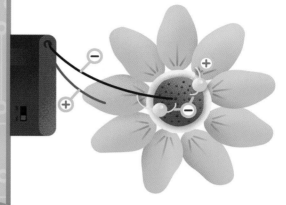

 **TEST YOUR CIRCUIT NOW!**

5 Shape a medium green ball into a leaf shape. Use a toothpick to press lines into the leaf.

6 Add the paper punch-outs around the LEDs to make a butterfly and a bee.

WHAT YOU'LL NEED:

- Orange clay
- White insulating clay
- 4 LEDs
- Paper punch-out: star

1 Roll two medium orange balls into thick snakes. Roll one end of each snake to make a long cone.

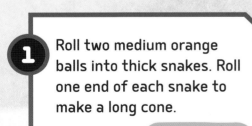

2 Roll a medium white ball into a long cone the same way you did in Step 1.

3 Split the legs of the LEDs to make Vs, with the positive ⊕ legs at the top and the negative ⊖ legs at the bottom. Press 4 LEDs into the white cone and smooth the clay over the legs to hide the slits.

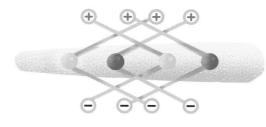

4 Press an orange cone onto the bottom of the white strip, covering the negative legs.

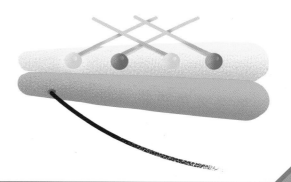

5 Press another orange cone onto the top of the positive legs. Attach the battery pack by sticking the red wire ⊕ into the top orange cone on the right. Poke the black wire ⊖ into the bottom orange cone on the left. Make sure the orange cones don't touch each other.

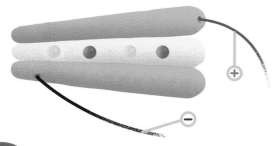

TEST YOUR CIRCUIT NOW!

6 Gently lift one end of the clay cones and nudge it lower to make a curve. Add the paper punch-out star and watch your shooting star glow.

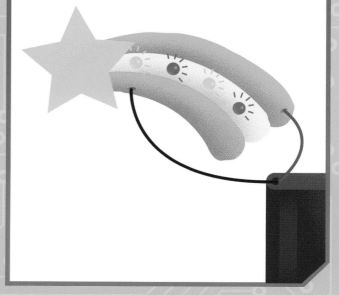

1 Shape 3 small green balls into flat diamonds. Use a toothpick to notch the diamonds' edges to make leaves. Roll tiny green balls into thin snakes and twist them to make vines. Arrange the leaves and vines to make a base, like this.

TIP: Make sure the leaves don't touch!

WHAT YOU'LL NEED:

- Green clay
- White insulating clay
- Orange clay
- Pencil and toothpick
- Green LED
- Paper punch-out: stem

2 Bend the LED legs to shorten them. Flatten a small white clay ball into a disk. Push the legs of the LED through the disk.

3 Push the longer, positive ⊕ LED leg into the leaf on the left. Insert the shorter, negative ⊖ leg into the leaf on the right. Attach the battery pack so the red wire is in the left leaf and the black wire is in the right leaf.

TEST YOUR CIRCUIT NOW!

4 To make the pumpkin, poke the eraser end of a pencil into a medium orange ball. Wiggle the eraser around inside to make the ball hollow with thin walls.

5 With the hole at the bottom, use a toothpick to poke through the pumpkin and gently carve out the jack-o'-lantern's eyes, nose, and mouth. If you want, press a toothpick into the sides of the pumpkin to make grooves.

6 Place the hollow pumpkin over the LED so that the light shines through. Insert the paper stem on top.

1 With a large ball of white clay, make a cylinder. Gently bend the longer, positive ⊕ LED leg into an L shape. Bend the shorter, negative ⊖ leg upward to make another L.

WHAT YOU'LL NEED:

- **White insulating clay**
- **Blue clay**
- **Yellow LED**
- **Paper punch-out: ON/OFF switch**
- **Optional: toothpick**

2 Press the LED into the top of the cylinder. The negative leg should poke up through the top. The positive leg should poke out the side.

3 Make a strip from a medium ball of blue clay. Poke the negative leg into the side of the strip, then wrap the strip around the top of the cylinder. Use your fingers to shape the blue clay into a cone.

4 Shape a small blue ball into a rectangle for the switch. Use a toothpick to make a groove across the middle. Place it over the end of the negative LED leg on the side of the handle.

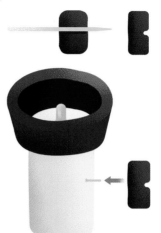

5 Attach the battery pack. Connect the red wire to the switch and the black wire to the cone.

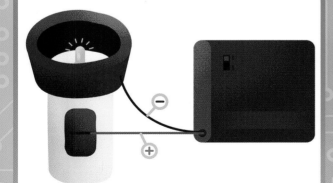

TEST YOUR CIRCUIT NOW!

6 Roll a thinner strip from a small blue ball and wrap it around the other end of the flashlight. Attach the paper ON/OFF switch.

TIP: Use a toothpick to add grooves to the bottom of the flashlight.

WHAT YOU'LL NEED:

- **White insulating clay**
- **Orange clay**
- **Blue clay**
- **Yellow LED**
- **Paper punch-outs: cupcake stand**
- **Optional: Toothpick**

1 Take the LED and gently bend the longer, positive ⊕ leg into an L shape. Cover the LED's legs with a small ball of white clay to make a candle, leaving about ¼ inch (6 mm) bare at the ends.

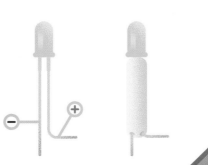

2 Take a medium orange clay ball and make a cup shape for the base. If you want, use a toothpick to make grooves around the sides of the base.

3 Flatten a small white clay ball into a pancake and place it on top of the base. Stick the negative LED leg into the center of the base—making sure it touches the orange cup underneath. The positive leg should rest on top of the white clay.

4 For frosting, roll a medium blue clay ball into a long snake. Wind the snake around the top of the base to make frosting. Make sure the frosting touches the positive LED leg on top of the white clay.

5 Attach the battery pack. Poke the black wire ⊖ into the cupcake base and the red wire ⊕ into the frosting. Make sure the frosting and cupcake base don't touch.

TEST YOUR CIRCUIT NOW!

6 Slide the cupcake stand together and place your cupcake on it. Add clay sprinkles or other decorations.

WHAT YOU'LL NEED:

- White insulating clay
- Green clay
- Black clay
- Orange clay
- 2 LEDs
- Paper punch-outs:
  2 stick arms

1 To make the head, first split the legs of two LEDs so they make straight lines. Press them into a medium white ball so that the negative ⊖ legs stick out the top and the positive ⊕ legs stick out the bottom of the ball. Smooth the clay over the cracks.

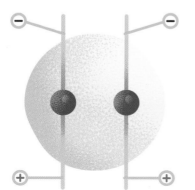

2 Flatten a small green ball into a disk. Place it on top of a large white clay ball. This is the body.

3 Make the hat. Roll a small black ball into a cylinder. Flatten a tiny black ball into a flat disk and place the cylinder on top.

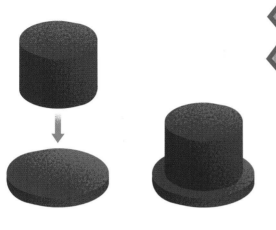

4 Push the LED legs sticking out of the bottom of the head into the green disk on the body. Slide the hat onto the wires at the top of the head.

5 Connect the battery pack by poking the black wire ⊖ into the hat and the red wire ⊕ into the green clay at the neck.

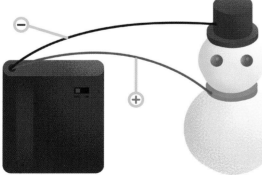

TEST YOUR CIRCUIT NOW!

6 Add the paper arms to your snowman. Use clay to make a carrot nose, a scarf, mouth, and buttons.

ASTRONAUT

WHAT YOU'LL NEED:

- Orange clay
- White insulating clay
- Black clay
- Dental floss
- 3 LEDs
- 2 toothpicks
- Paper punch-outs:
  2 astronaut arms

1 For the body, shape a large orange ball into a thick square. Use a piece of dental floss to cut the square in half diagonally.

2 Shape a small white ball into a thin strip. Place it between the halves of the body. Make sure that the orange halves don't touch each other.

3 Poke the longer, positive ⊕ legs of the LEDs into the left side of the body. Push the shorter, negative ⊖ legs into the right side of the body.

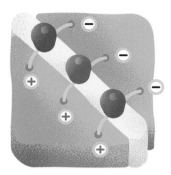

4 Attach the battery pack. The red wire ⊕ should go into the left side of the body. The black wire ⊖ should go into the right side of the body.

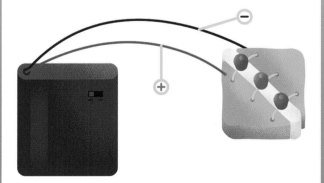

TEST YOUR CIRCUIT NOW!

5 To make each leg, stack two small white balls and two medium orange balls as shown. A white ball should be on top.

6. Ask a grown-up to cut a toothpick in half. Stick one half of the toothpick into the clay balls of each leg to hold them together. The end of the toothpick should stick out of the top of each leg.

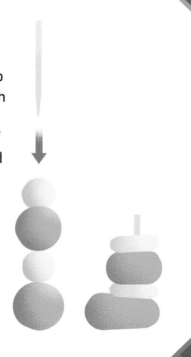

7. Place the body on top of the legs, pressing it into the ends of the toothpicks.

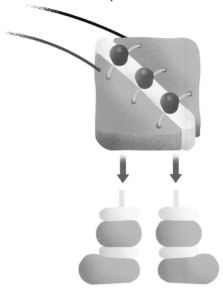

8. To make the helmet, flatten a tiny black clay ball into a rectangle. Press the rectangle onto a small orange ball.

9. Cut another toothpick in half. Insert one half of the toothpick halfway into the top of the body. Then push the head onto the other end of the toothpick.

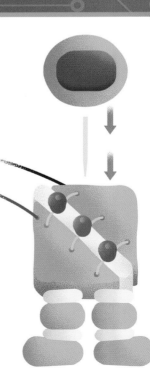

10 Add the paper arms and flag to complete your astronaut.

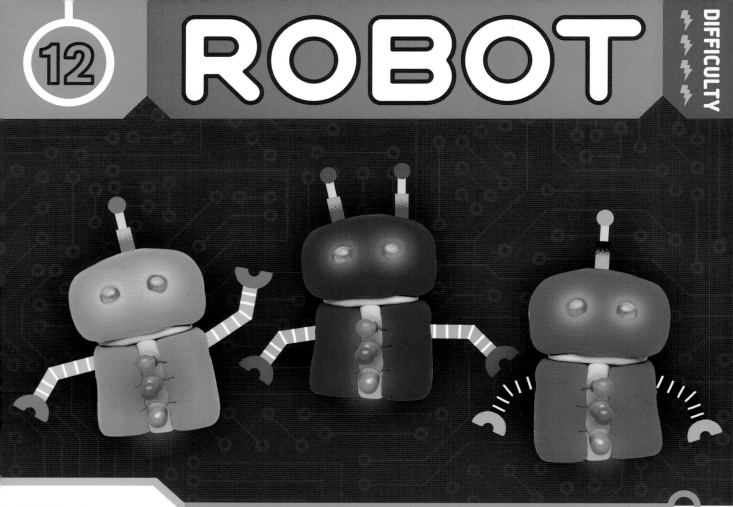

WHAT YOU'LL NEED:

- Blue clay
- White insulating clay
- Dental floss
- 5 LEDs
- Paper punch-outs:
  2 robot arms, robot
  antenna

1 For the body, roll a large ball of blue clay into a cylinder. Cut the cylinder in half, top to bottom, with dental floss.

2 Shape a small white clay ball into a thin rectangle. Place it between the body halves, making sure the halves don't touch.

3 Insert three LEDs into the front of the body, with the positive legs in the left half and the negative legs in the right half. Connect the red wire ⊕ to the left side of the body and the black wire ⊖ to the right side of the body.

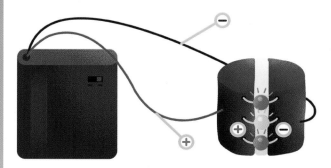

TEST YOUR CIRCUIT NOW!

4 Flatten a small white clay ball into a disc and place it on top of the body.

TIP: If you want your robot's eyes to light up, follow Steps 5–11. If you want a simple bot, just make a head out of clay, place it on top of the body, and skip to Step 12.

5 Take two LEDs and split the legs so they form a V shape. The positive legs ⊕ should be on the left side, and the negative ⊖ legs on the right side.

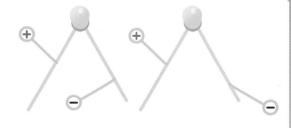

6 For the head, take a medium white clay ball and press it so that the bottom is flat.

7 Press the LEDs into the front of the head so that the legs stick out of the bottom. Move the positive legs so that they both come out of the left side. Move the negative legs so that they both come out of the right side. Smooth the clay to cover any cracks.

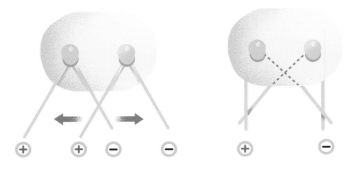

8 Flatten a medium ball of blue clay into a thin sheet. You'll use this sheet to cover the head.

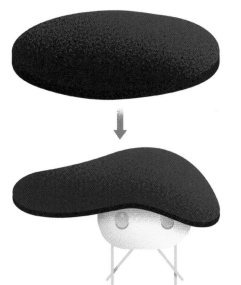

9 Cover the head with the sheet of blue clay, including the LED bulbs. Wrap the sheet so that it just covers the bottom edges of the head. Don't let the sheet touch the LED legs.

10 Use your fingers to push the bulbs of the LEDs through the blue sheet. Smooth any wrinkles or bumps in the blue clay.

11 Place the head on the body. Push the LED legs on the left side of the head into the left side of the body, through the white clay. Push the LEDs on the right side of the head into the right side of the body.

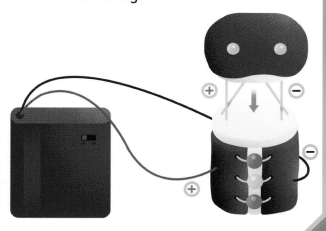

12 Add the paper arms and an antenna to finish up your robot.

WHAT YOU'LL NEED:

- Black clay
- White insulating clay
- Green clay
- Orange clay
- 2 LEDs
- Paper punch-outs: 2 crosspanes, moon

1 Use two medium black clay balls and one medium white clay ball to make three thin squares of the same size.

2 To make stars, bend the LEDs so that the positive legs ⊕ are horizontal. Push the negative ⊖ legs through the white square, keeping the positive legs on top of the clay.

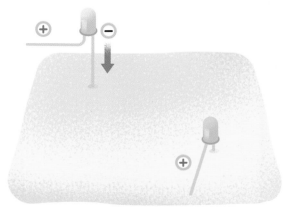

3 Bend the negative LED legs so that they lie flat against the bottom of the white square. Place one of the black squares under the white square.

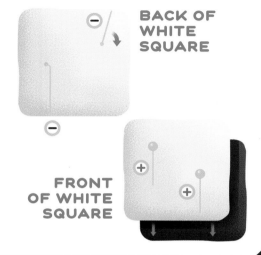

BACK OF WHITE SQUARE

FRONT OF WHITE SQUARE

4 Place the other black square on top of the white square and the LED bulbs. Poke the LED bulbs through the black clay, then smooth the black clay around the bulbs.

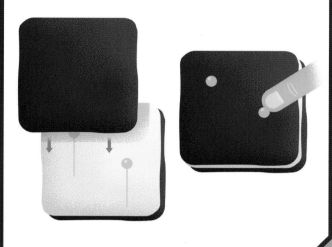

5 Attach the battery pack. The red wire should connect to the top black layer, and the black wire should connect to the bottom black layer. Make sure the two black layers don't touch.

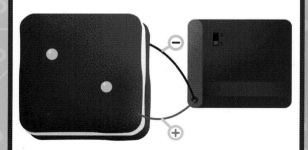

TEST YOUR CIRCUIT NOW!

6 Press the paper crosspane and the moon onto the clay. Use two small green balls to make two thin sheets for curtains. Add polka dots with orange clay.

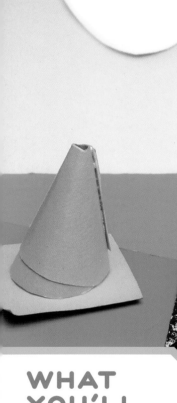

WHAT YOU'LL NEED:

- Black clay
- White insulating clay
- Dental floss
- 2 LEDs (red and blue)
- Paper punch-outs:
  4 wheels, headlights

1 For the body, shape a large black clay ball into rectangular block. Cut the block in half with dental floss as shown.

2 Flatten a small white ball to make a thin square. Place the square between the two halves of the body. Set this piece aside.

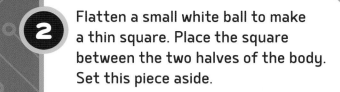

3 Shape a large white clay ball into a rounded cube, like a marshmallow. Gently press it against the table to give it four flat sides.

4 Split the legs of the LEDs into V shapes, with the positive ⊕ legs on the left and the negative ⊖ legs on the right.

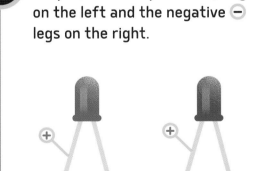

5 Push the red LED through the white cube so the legs go all the way through. The positive ⊕ LED leg should be on the left side, the negative ⊖ leg on the right side. Repeat with the blue LED.

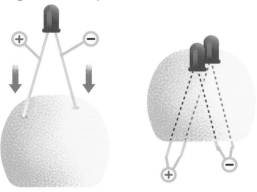

TIP: If the LED legs don't poke through, pull some white clay off of the bottom to make the cube shorter.

6 Place the dome on top of the body you made in Step 2. Make sure the positive ⊕ LED legs poke into the left side. Poke the end of the negative ⊖ LED legs into the right side.

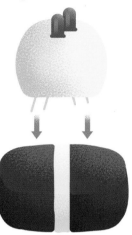

7 Attach the battery pack. Plug the red wire ⊕ into the left side of the body. Plug the black wire ⊖ into the right side of the body.

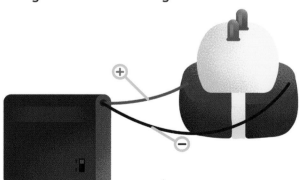

TEST YOUR CIRCUIT NOW!

8 Roll four thin, short snakes from tiny balls of black clay. Place these on the corners of the dome. Make sure the ends of the snakes do not touch the body.

9 Shape a tiny ball of black into a small square for the roof. Place it on top of the LED lights.

10 Use your finger to push the LED bulbs through the black clay. Pat down the roof to make it smooth.

11 Attach the paper wheels and the headlights to your car.

WHAT YOU'LL NEED:

- Orange clay
- White insulating clay
- Green clay
- Toothpick
- 3 LEDs (2 green, 1 red)
- Pencil
- Paper punch-outs:
  2 horns, 2 ears, 2 arms,
  2 wings, tail tip

1 For a belly, shape a flattened triangle from a medium ball of orange clay. Use a toothpick to make grooves.

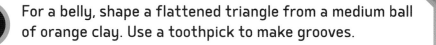

2 To make each leg, flatten a small orange ball into a disk. Pinch the edge of the disk to make a foot.

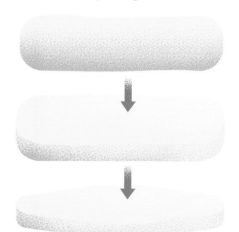

3 Press the legs onto the sides of the belly.

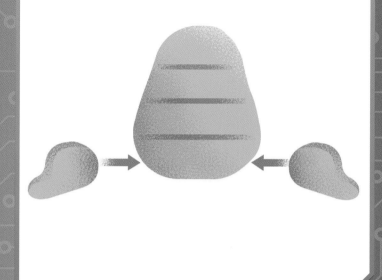

4 Roll a thick snake from a large white ball. Flatten the snake to make a strip as wide as the belly. Pinch the ends of the strip to make them pointy.

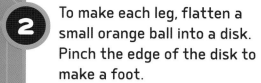

5 Place the white clay on top of the belly to make a chin and a tail.

6 Curl in the shorter, negative ⊖ legs of the LEDs. Poke the longer positive ⊕ legs through the white clay and into the orange clay for the eyes and mouth.

7 Roll a long cone from a large ball of green clay. Flatten the cone into a thin, long teardrop.

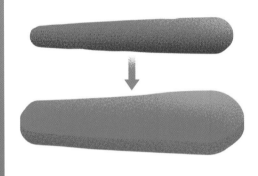

8 Use the point of a pencil to poke two holes in the round end of the green clay. This is where the LEDs will poke through for the dragon's eyes.

9 Lay the teardrop shape over the white clay strip. Line up the holes in the clay with the LED bulbs and poke them through.

10 Attach your battery pack. Connect the red wire ⊕ to the orange clay at the neck and the black wire ⊖ to the green clay near the head.

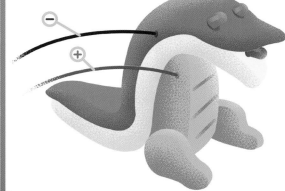

TEST YOUR CIRCUIT NOW!

11 Use your fingers to shape the head and the square snout of the dragon. Add two tiny green clay balls to the nose. Use the tip of a pencil to make holes for the nostrils.

12 Add the paper horns, ears, wings, arms, and tail tip to your dragon.

CREDITS

Editor: F. S. Kim

Designers: Lizzy Doyle, Andrea Miller, and April Chorba

Technical illustrator: Ian Dickens

Photographer: Ken Karp

Stylist: Adrianna Youngren

Buyer: Vicky Eva and Kelly Shaffer

Managing editor: Barrie Zipkin

Packaging designer: Owen Keating

Crafters: Kristin Carder, Lizzy Doyle, Elizabeth Dyer, Caitlin Harpin, Owen Keating, Hannah Rogge, Lesley Thelander, Sam Walker, and Adrianna Youngren

Special thanks to: Stacy Lellos, Netta Rabin, Hannah Rogge, and April Chorba

Get creative with more from KLUTZ

Looking for more goof-proof activities, sneak peeks, and giveaways? Find us online!

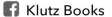 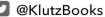